MEGATECH

Alien Lifesearch

Quest for extraterrestrial organisms

David Jefferis

Crabtree

Introduction

U ntil a few years ago, the idea of ETs, or extraterrestrials, was all science fiction. Alien life was thought about as likely as Martian invaders or monsters from the movies.

Today however, the idea of life on other worlds has moved closer to reality. In 1996, the United States space agency, NASA, showed a chunk of space rock, a meteorite that some scientists believe contains fossils of past life on Mars, the Red Planet.

Discoveries of new worlds far off in space, and closer looks at those nearer to the Earth, have led many scientists to hope that soon they will find life on other planets.

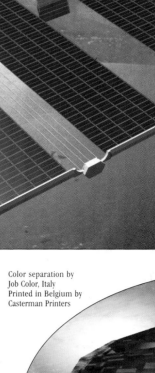

Crabtree Publishing Company

PMB 16A   612 Welland Ave
350 Fifth Ave   St. Catharines, ON
Ste. 3308   Canada L2M 5V6
New York
NY 10118

234567 Printed in Belgium 76543210

Edited by
Norman Barrett
Coordinating editor
Ellen Rodger
Consulting editor
Virginia Mainprize
Technical consultants
Mat Irvine FBIS
Doug Millard, The Science Museum,
London

Picture research by
David Pratt
Created and produced by
Alpha Communications in association
with Firecrest Books Ltd.

©1999 Alpha Communications and
©1999 Firecrest Books Ltd.

Cataloging-in-Publication Data
Jefferis, David.
    Alien life search: quest for
extraterrestrial organisms
        p. cm. -- (Megatech)
    Includes index.
    Summary: Discusses what other
planets may have the right conditions
to support life and surveys aliens,
unidentified flying objects, and our
exploration of space.

ISBN 0-7787-0049-6 (rlb). --
ISBN 0-7787-0059-3(paper)
    1. Life on other planets -- Juvenile
literature. 2. Galaxies -- Juvenile
literature. 3. Exobiology -- Juvenile
literature.
[1. Life on other planets.
2. Extraterrestrial beings. 3. Outer
space -- Exploration.] I. Title. II. Series.
QB54.J44 1999
516.8'39--dc21 LC 98-45355
CIP AC

Pictures on these pages, clockwise
from far left:
1 Possible Martian microbes, shown
by the U.S. Space Agency, NASA, in
1996.
2 International Space Station in Earth
orbit, likely base for some future life
search operations.
3 'Gray' extraterrestrial, supposed
pilot of a crashed spacecraft, in 1947.
4 The planet Saturn. A space probe
will explore Saturn's big moon Titan, in
2004, to search for signs of life.
5 Distant gas clouds, with new stars
forming inside. In the far future there
may be planets, and living things, too.
6 Many people think aliens have
visited the Earth, flying in advanced
spacecraft, popularly known as UFOs.

Previous page shows:
Artist's idea of an alien flying creature.

Color separation by
Job Color, Italy
Printed in Belgium by
Casterman Printers

Contents

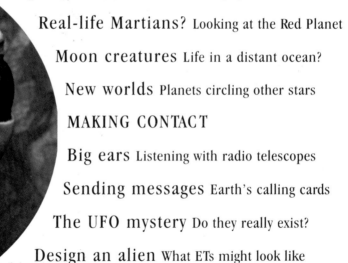

This vast universe

▲ *Galileo was the first to spot the four biggest moons of Jupiter. He saw Saturn's rings too. However, his telescopes were not powerful enough to make out exactly what they were.*

W ith a universe as large as ours, some scientists think there might be life on other planets, somewhere in deep space.

For thousands of years, people have watched the moon and stars in the night sky. Some 'stars' that moved from night to night were called planets, after the Greek word for 'wanderers.'

It was when Galileo Galilei and other astronomers – people who study the stars – started observing the night skies that the idea of Earth being just one planet in the Sun's family of planets was first put forward. Galileo watched the movement of stars and planets through a telescope. He confirmed that instead of the Sun revolving around the Earth, the Earth and other planets revolved around the Sun. The idea upset many people, and Galileo was threatened with torture for his beliefs.

▶ *The 'Inhabitant of the Dog Star' (top) and 'Moon Creature' were thought up by an artist in the 1700s.*

▲ *One of Galileo's telescopes, in Florence, Italy, where the astronomer lived and worked for many years.*

B y the late 1800s, astronomers were exploring the night sky with more powerful telescopes. Most of the planets in our Solar System had been found, except distant Pluto, which was not spotted until 1930.

In the 1920s, U.S. astronomer Edwin Hubble showed that our galaxy, the Milky Way, itself a vast spiral group of about 100 billion stars, was just one of countless others. People who believe in alien life claim that, with such a large universe, there must be life on some planets circling other stars.

▲ *Scientists think that stars and planets form from clouds of dust and gas.*

▶ With powerful equipment, astronomers can view galaxies 12 to 15 billion light years away. Each galaxy contains about 100 billion stars, so there could be lots of planets out there.

▲ Scientists pose for the camera in 1931. Edwin Hubble is second from left. Albert Einstein, the famous mathematician, is third from right.

◀ This beautiful galaxy gave Edwin Hubble an idea of the size of space. On the night of October 5, 1923, he took a photo of a misty patch of light in the sky. In the photo, Hubble noticed a type of star, a 'Cepheid variable,' that let him measure the galaxy's distance from Earth. He worked out it was a million light-years away from Earth.

The Andromeda galaxy is thought to be quite similar to our own spiral Milky Way galaxy

Planet Earth is the only place where we definitely know there are living things. We can only gaze into the night sky and guess what other life might be out there. In the rest of our Solar System, the planets, moons, rocks and dust that move around the Sun, no definite signs of life have yet been found. Space scientists are still searching for simple organisms in space.

What is a light-year?

A light-year is a unit used by astronomers to measure distances between the stars. It is simply the distance traveled by light in one year. At about 186,000 miles (300,000 km) per second, this is a distance of nearly 6 million million miles.

Our nearest star, the Sun, is just over eight light-minutes from Earth. In other words, light from the Sun takes just over eight minutes to reach us. The nearest star to the Solar System is Proxima Centauri, which lies just over four light-years away.

Origins of life

L ife seems to have appeared on Earth billions of years ago. Whether it exists anywhere else is still unknown.

It is not certain when or how life forms first began on Earth. The earliest living things are thought to have appeared about four billion years ago. This was long after the Sun and planets had formed from swirling clouds of dust and gas, the remains of stars that had exploded far away in space.

▲ *Stars are born in the heart of clouds of gas. Eventually, enough matter collects to set off the nuclear fusion reactions that are needed to produce 'sunpower.'*

Tails of gas and dust

Coma of gas and dust released as comet approaches Sun and outer layers of nucleus boil away in Sun's heat

Nucleus is a 'dirty snowball' of frozen ice, dust, and rocks

▲ *Comets contain organic molecules believed to be building blocks of life. In the early Solar System many comets collided with the newly formed planets*

If you could time-travel back to early Earth, you would see chunks of space dust, ice, and rock, in the form of comets and meteors, smashing into our world. You could watch volcanoes pumping out gases and water vapor to form an atmosphere. You might paddle in warm, shallow seas, rich in hydrogen and other chemicals. It is in these 'soupy' seas that the building blocks of life, amino acids and proteins, began to form into living organisms capable of reproducing themselves.

O ver time, a process called evolution forced living things to change and grow. This change resulted in the development of microbes, plants, primitive fish, and reptiles, and later the plants and animals of today. These same life processes may have happened on other planets such as Mars and Venus, which are rocky worlds not unlike Earth in their make-up.

At some point, the climate changed on these planets. Today, Mars is cold and dry, while Venus roasts at furnace heat. This leaves Earth as the only known center of life in the Solar System.

► *The single cell is the simplest form of life on Earth. All living things are based on this basic unit.*

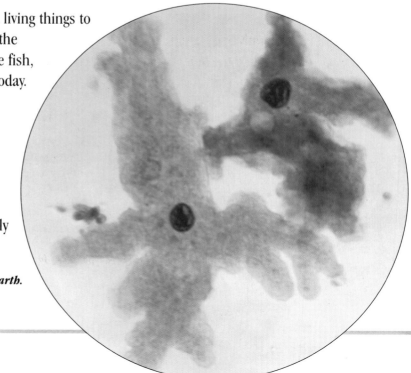

Chunks of space rock crash into shallow seas on Earth billions of years ago. In the sky, the Moon glows with the heat of many, much bigger, strikes.

There are three main theories, or ideas, about the beginnings of life on Earth. The first is the 'ball of ice' idea, in which life started under thick ice, a protection against deadly ultraviolet radiation from the hot Sun. In the 'warm water' theory, life began in small ponds or lakes, with simple organisms, or life forms, such as bacteria. The third theory describes the 'hot saucepan,' where life started in places such as hot geysers and volcanic areas.

Another idea is that simple life forms were brought to Earth by comets and meteors that crashed against the planet.

If any or all of these theories are correct – and if planets form in similar ways across the universe – then life might have evolved on planets of other stars like the Sun. There may be millions of life-bearing planets out in space.

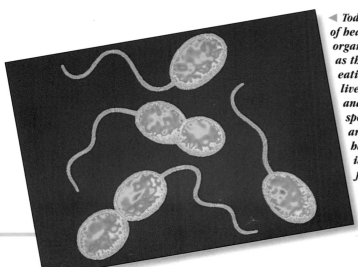

Today, all sorts of heat-loving organisms, such as these sulfur-eating bacteria, live in geysers and other hot spots. Such areas may have been ideal for the first living things.

How many living things are there on planet Earth?

The Earth is home to about 1.75 million known species of animals and plants, a number that has changed many times in the past.

The extinction of entire plant and animal populations resulted from natural disasters or changes in climate.

One well-known example of exctinction of a species is the disappearance of the dinosaurs about 65 million years ago. Many experts think that an explosion and the resulting dust clouds caused by a huge meteor crashing into Central America, caused the dinosaurs to die out.

Children of the Sun

U ntil space probes explored the Solar System, it seemed possible that we would find life on the planets nearest to Earth.

The 'ecosphere' is a name given to the zone around the Sun where conditions are thought to be suitable for life. Earth is in the center of the ecosphere where the temperatures are just right. Closer to the Sun, it is too hot. Farther out, it is too cold. Until the 1960s, the two planets thought most likely to have life were Earth's nearest neighbors in space, Venus and Mars.

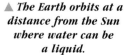

▲ *The Earth orbits at a distance from the Sun where water can be a liquid.*

▲ *Space probes have given us information about other planets and locations where life might exist in the Solar System.*

M any early science fiction writers used Mars and Venus as settings for their stories. The English author H.G. Wells wrote about octopus-like Martians in his Earth-invasion novel, War of the Worlds. Later, U.S. writer Edgar Rice Burroughs, in his Barsoom adventure books, described Mars as a planet with all sorts of weird and wonderful creatures. Even professional astronomers thought life on Mars was possible. Through their telescopes some thought they saw changing patterns, which they believed could be plant growth. However, space probes of the 1960s revealed a cold and dry desert planet. Viking landers of the 1970s confirmed that there were no 'little green men' running around Mars.

◄ *A tentacled Martian invader coming out of its spacecraft, gives an Earthling a shock in a scene from 'War of the Worlds.'*

I deas about conditions on Venus, a planet closer to the Sun than Earth, ranged from steamy jungles to hot deserts. One science fiction story featured oceans of bubbling oil. The 1950s comic-strip hero Dan Dare battled the evil Mekon on a Venus that was in some ways not unlike Earth. Even the wildest science fiction stories did not imagine the grim reality recorded by the Venera space probes. The probes, launched by the USSR in the 1970s, revealed a planet with clouds of sulfuric acid and temperatures hotter than an oven. The atmospheric pressure alone would crush humans to a lifeless smear.

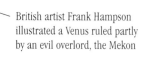

British artist Frank Hampson illustrated a Venus ruled partly by an evil overlord, the Mekon

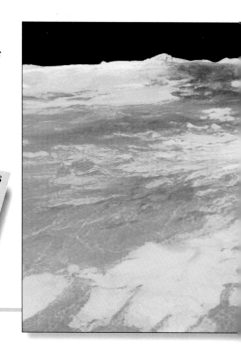

EDGAR RICE BURROUGHS

CARSON OF VENUS

An Earthman in a world of unearthly perils

The Venus of Edgar Rice Burroughs novels had many monsters

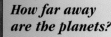

How far away are the planets?

Space is BIG. If you think of the Earth-Sun distance of 92.6 million miles (149 million km) as about 1 in (2.5 cm), then Mars orbits the Sun at 1.6 in (4 cm) distant, while Pluto freezes 40 in (100 cm) out. This distance is nothing, however, compared to the gulfs between the stars. On the same scale, the nearest star, Proxima Centauri, is nearly 4.3 miles (7 km) away.

◄ *A family portrait of the Solar System. The planets are shown with their moons and the massive Sun behind.*

From nearest the Sun to farthest out, the planets are:

1 *Mercury*
2 *Venus*
3 *Earth*
4 *Mars*
5 *Jupiter*
6 *Saturn*
7 *Uranus*
8 *Neptune*
9 *Pluto*

For clarity, the inner planets (1-4) are shown bigger in scale than the outer worlds. Shrink them eight times to get the scale correct.

◄ *The hills of Venus, as viewed by radar equipment that sees through the planet's thick clouds.*

Mercury is an airless, lifeless, cratered planet nearest to the Sun. Jupiter, the fifth planet from the Sun, has a moon called Europa that is thought to have oceans under an icy crust. Europa is a target for a lifesearch. Saturn's moon Titan may possibly have some microscopic organisms, or tiny life forms. Further out into the Solar System, temperatures are too cold for life as we know it to survive. On Pluto, the planet farthest from the Sun, a summer's day is −380°F (−230°C).

Explorers from Earth

Space probes have landed on or flown by all the planets in the Solar System except Pluto. In the 1970s, instruments were devised to test for signs of life on the planet Mars.

Robot missions to the planets started in 1964, with the launch of the Mariner 4 space probe (shown at left) to Mars. The windmill-shaped craft sent back photographs of craters and dusty plains, which forever changed our view of Mars.

▲ *On their return to Earth, astronauts on early Moon flights were checked to make sure they did not bring back any alien microbes.*

Later space probes showed other features of Mars, including volcanoes and canyons, but no signs of life. In 1976, two Viking probes landed on Mars. Each probe carried a mini-laboratory to check conditions such as wind, weather, and temperature, and to hunt for life.

Samples of Martian soil were scooped up for testing. Three major experiments, controlled from Earth, checked for living organisms. There were some unusual instrument readings but no real clear-cut signs of Martian life. Most scientists agreed that chemical reactions alone could have caused some of the unusual readings.

Scoop at end of arm collects soil for mini-laboratory

▲ *Viking probes had orbiter sections that mapped Mars from above. One lander from each orbiter touched down on flat Martian regions.*

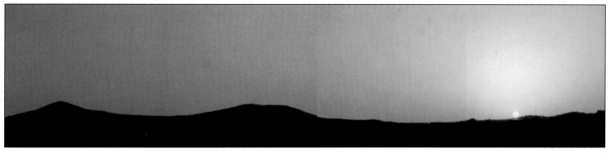

◄ *Clear skies and a chilly sunset on Mars, as pictured by Sojourner's cameras at the end of 24 days on the Red Planet.*

Solar panels on roof

Six wheels for crossing rough ground

► *Sojourner bounced to a landing inside a cluster of air bags. Here they are tested on Earth before flight.*

► *When it was built, the Sojourner rover weighed 25.3 lb (11.5 kg). On Mars, a smaller planet than Earth, with lower gravity, the rover weighed barely 9.7 lb (4.4 kg).*

Instrument to check makeup of rock

◄ *A ramp led down to the Martian surface. Here the rover peeks at a rock the science team named 'Yogi'.*

Model of a future Mars rover. TV cameras are on the pole

In 1997, Mars was once again the center of attention as a U.S. probe approached the Red Planet. Using giant balloons to cushion the shock of landing, the probe touched down safely. On board was a small rover vehicle.

The rover, called Sojourner, found rounded pebbles that looked as if they had been made smooth by running water. This suggests that Mars was a warmer planet in the past. If there were rivers, future probes may find fossils of Martian lifeforms.

How do you drive a Mars rover?

The Sojourner rover – nicknamed 'Rocky' – was just 25.5 in (65 cm) long. It traveled to the planet in 1997 inside a Pathfinder lander. Rocky's driver was NASA engineer Brian Cooper, who plotted the vehicle's route using a computer screen and joystick back on Earth.

Wearing 3D glasses that gave depth to images arriving on Earth from Rocky's video camera (signals took about 15 minutes), Cooper tackled many problems. These included Rocky going in circles, trying to climb a boulder and getting stuck in a crack. Even so, the solar-powered vehicle was very successful, lasting nearly three months instead of the planned seven days.

In the end, the chilly -13°F (-25°C) autumn nights of Mars became too much for Rocky. An emergency battery went flat, the solar panels were covered with dust, and the little rover fell silent.

Real-life Martians?

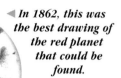

Mars, the 'Red Planet,' has long been a favorite target in the search for extraterrestrial, or alien, life.

▲ *These winged Martians are from a 1903 magazine.*

About a hundred years ago, some astronomers thought they saw canals on Mars. This led to the idea that a now-dead civilization, or society, had dug vast channels from icy polar regions to carry water into the deserts. One astronomer, American Percival Lowell, even drew detailed maps of the planet with canals marked on them. It turned out, however, that the canals existed only in Lowell's imagination. The first space probes sent to Mars revealed a cold, dry, cratered world, with no canals in sight.

▶ *Early looks at Mars were limited by the quality of telescope. Few details could be seen, even on clear nights.*

Prima Martis facies
M.
Occ. — Oric
S.
Primæ faciei
Succeſſiua conuersio

◀ *In 1862, this was the best drawing of the red planet that could be found.*

▲ *Lowell's canal-filled map of Mars.*

Mars used to be warmer and wetter than it is now. Pictures show what look like dried-up river valleys and an ancient ocean. With the Solar System's biggest volcano (Olympus Mons) and a rift valley (Valles Marineris) that dwarfs anything on Earth, Mars is a fascinating place.

Now, what about the rumored 'face on Mars'? Some people claimed it was a giant Martian rock carving, but 1998 photos showed it was a natural formation. Near the 'face' is a structure called the 'city,' for its regular crisscross rock groupings.

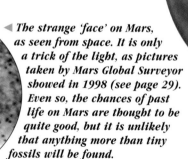

◀ *The strange 'face' on Mars, as seen from space. It is only a trick of the light, as pictures taken by Mars Global Surveyor showed in 1998 (see page 29). Even so, the chances of past life on Mars are thought to be quite good, but it is unlikely that anything more than tiny fossils will be found.*

◀ *Author H.G. Wells invented Martian invaders in his 1890s book 'War of the Worlds.' These 'war machines' are from a 1953 movie, based on the Wells story.*

▶ *In 1996, claims were made that tiny life forms (shown in blue) seemed to be imbedded in space rock found in Antarctica. It was a piece of Martian rock, 'splashed' off that planet by an ancient meteor hit.*

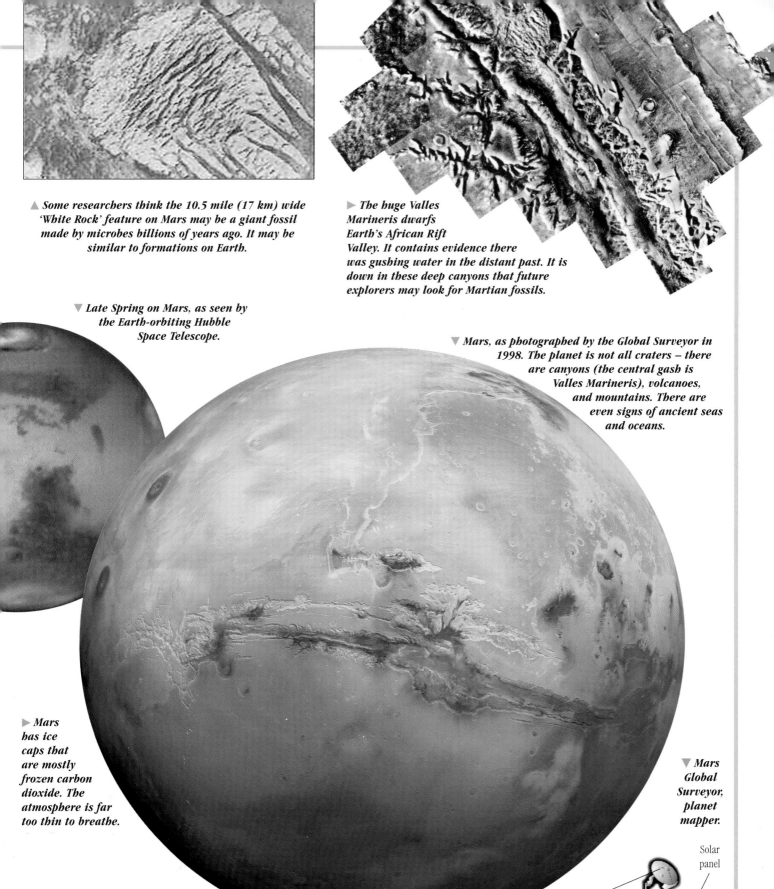

▲ Some researchers think the 10.5 mile (17 km) wide 'White Rock' feature on Mars may be a giant fossil made by microbes billions of years ago. It may be similar to formations on Earth.

▶ The huge Valles Marineris dwarfs Earth's African Rift Valley. It contains evidence there was gushing water in the distant past. It is down in these deep canyons that future explorers may look for Martian fossils.

▼ Late Spring on Mars, as seen by the Earth-orbiting Hubble Space Telescope.

▼ Mars, as photographed by the Global Surveyor in 1998. The planet is not all craters – there are canyons (the central gash is Valles Marineris), volcanoes, and mountains. There are even signs of ancient seas and oceans.

▶ Mars has ice caps that are mostly frozen carbon dioxide. The atmosphere is far too thin to breathe.

▼ Mars Global Surveyor, planet mapper.

Solar panel

Communications antenna

Moon creatures

Scientists who search for life on other planets are fascinated by Europa, a moon of Jupiter, the Solar System's biggest planet. Saturn's moon Titan may also have some simple forms of life in its cloudy, orange-tinted atmosphere.

Life on a frozen moon might seem unlikely. Although a search for life would normally be made somewhere closer to the Sun, Europa is now thought to be a reasonable site to investigate. Its surface is covered with thick ice, but space probes have shown that there could be oceans of water under the ice, warmed by tidal energy from Jupiter. Huge chunks of ice have pushed up through Europa's surface, before freezing solid. No signs of life have yet been found on Jupiter's moon, but discoveries on Earth have led scientists to believe that life might exist in Europa's oceans.

▲ The Galileo space probe flew close to Europa in 1998. It revealed this weird landscape, full of crisscross cracks in the ice.

▼ Volcanoes bubbling away at the bottom of Earth's oceans provide minerals and warmth for simple forms of life. Many creatures live around these hot spots, at water pressures that would squash humans to a pulp.

▲ The huge gas giant Jupiter, compared with blue planet Earth (yellow arrow) and Jupiter's ice-coated moon Europa (white arrow).

What is tidal energy?

The force of gravity between the Earth and the Moon causes ocean tides on Earth. It is possible to use some of this energy. Power stations, such as the one at the River Rance estuary, in France, have been built. Water gushes through channels in a dam to spin turbines that can generate electricity.

On Europa, the pull from nearby Jupiter is far more powerful, resulting in massive 'moonquakes,' with grinding rocks creating heat. As a result, Europa may be warm enough to have oceans under its surface.

◄ *An illustration of what it may look like under Europa's ice. A lander has drilled a hole through the ice and released a mini-submarine to explore the water. This scene could be reality in the 2000s. Exploration of Europa might confirm that simple forms of life exist on this far-off moon.*

Sadly, future visitors to Jupiter's moons will not see the tropical paradise shown on this 1928 sci-fi magazine

▼ *Saturn is the planet with beautiful rings and lots of moons, too. The biggest is Titan, another possible home for life. Its clouds contain chemicals and water vapor, similar to gases on Earth when life began.*

U ntil recently, it was thought that light was needed to provide basic energy for living things. Earth's ocean bottoms were thought to be mostly lifeless, and the idea of creatures living deep underground was out of the question. However, many creatures have been found around the vents (openings) of volcanoes on the ocean floor. Even more surprisingly, bacteria and simple organisms have been found in rock cracks deep below ground. The main thing that lets these creatures, named 'intra-terrestrials,' thrive seems to be heat. Heat gives them the raw energy needed to survive.

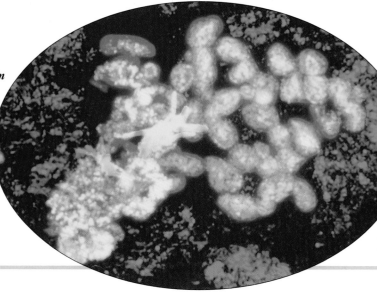

► *Living in cracks in the hot rocks far below the surface of the Earth are tiny organisms that use underground heat for energy.*

R esearchers say that, if life can thrive in these conditions on Earth, why not in an ocean of Europa, a moon nearly 3100 miles (5000 km) in diameter?

In the future, a robot probe could be launched with a lander and a mini-sub to crack through the ice and explore for life in Europa's oceans.

New worlds

The idea of strange planets orbiting stars other than our Sun used to be pure fantasy. Now planet-hunting scientists have changed this gripping science-fiction idea to hard science fact.

▲ *Before planet discoveries came dust ring photographs. This image shows a dust ring around the star Beta Pictoris, first seen in the 1980s. Planets will eventually form from the ring of tiny particles.*

No one has yet confirmed a new Earth-like planet out there, but the search continues. In 1991, astronomer Alex Wolszczan tracked down two mystery objects circling a tiny star in the constellation of Virgo. His discovery, the first planets seen around a star other than the Sun, was confirmed three years later. However, the star pours out so much deadly radiation that anything alive would be killed in moments.

◄ *Orbiting in space, the Hubble Space Telescope, shown here in a Space Shuttle cargo bay, carries out research above the distorting effects of Earth's swirling atmosphere. As useful as Hubble is, a lot of research is still carried out in observatories on Earth.*

In 1995, another planet was discovered, this time orbiting a star called 51 Pegasi. The planet is mysterious. According to present theories of the formation of planets, it seems to be too near to its parent star. It is a large planet and should be as gassy as Jupiter. However, the radiation from 51 Pegasi may have blown away most of the planet's gases, leaving a huge, exposed rocky core.

??? How do they find new planets?

Optical telescopes are not powerful enough to show visible images of planets of other stars, so astronomers try to spot them by measuring the 'wobble' of a star.

Just as our Moon's gravitational pull affects the ocean tides of a much larger Earth, a planet can affect the movement of a much larger star. Detecting these tiny movements is the target for planet-hunting astronomers.

From the amount of movement, experts can make good guesses about the size and nature of the planet, brown dwarf, or other sub-stellar object.

▶ *The planet that orbits 51 Pegasi may look like this. It is near its parent star (shown behind it) and 'roasts' at about 2400°F (1300°C). Its 'year' (the time to complete a single orbit) takes just four Earth days!*

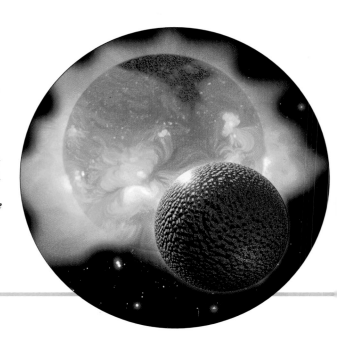

◄ Who knows what wonders and mysteries are out there, waiting to be discovered. Planets with three moons or more may be just one of the exotic sights for future galaxy sightseers.

In 1996, a giant planet of the star 70 Virginis was discovered by a team led by U.S. scientists Geoffrey Marcy and R. Paul Butler. It was the first planet thought to have a reasonable surface temperature. Marcy calculated this to be about 175°F (80°C), "about the temperature of warm milk." It is still too hot for humans to enjoy, however – a warm summer's day on most of Earth is about 85°F (30°C).

Special telescopes that are now being planned may detect life using a spectroscope, which can reveal chemicals in an atmosphere. As one scientist puts it, "We are not talking about discovering animal life directly, but we would be able to see if there was oxygen or ozone that could only be produced by life. We would also be able to see if there were seas and grass present."

After 51 Pegasi, several other planet discoveries have been made, although most star companions found so far are not really planets. They are called 'brown dwarfs.' Brown dwarfs are much bigger than normal planets, yet are not hot enough to burn as a star.

Will astronomers find a new Earth? More sensitive equipment is needed, but most experts think that Earth-like planets will be found someday soon. Then, lifesearchers may be close to success. The best guesses put such a discovery some years away, perhaps around 2015 to 2020, so just wait and see!

▲ This telescope is one of several designs for an upgraded replacement for today's Hubble telescope. Plans are also being made for deep-space telescopes to float in orbit beyond Jupiter. Viewing would then be clear of the dust particles found in the inner Solar System.

Big ears

▲ *SETI pioneer Dr. Frank Drake, under the metal bowl of the Arecibo radio telescope in Puerto Rico.*

Looking for new planets is one thing, finding intelligent ETs (extraterrestrials) is something else. Some people on Earth hope to pick up radio signals beamed toward our planet by such ETs.

In 1960, U.S. astronomer Frank Drake aimed a radio telescope receiver at two nearby stars to listen for any radio signals that might be broadcast by alien civilizations. Drake's Project Ozma was based on his idea that in our Milky Way galaxy of 100 billion suns, there might be some planets with aliens who use radio waves like we do on Earth. This was the first search for extraterrestrial intelligence (SETI). Since then there have been many further attempts.

▲ *Any galaxy could be home to hundreds of advanced civilizations if Drake's ideas are correct.*

For his first Project Ozma experiments, Frank Drake used this radio telescope

Listening to the stars is not quite so simple as it sounds. Problems include: Where do you point your radio telescope? Is your receiver sensitive enough? Do you have enough money to buy and maintain the equipment?

What is the Drake equation?

$$N = R * Fp \ Np \ Fl \ Fi \ Fc \ L$$

This strange-looking letter group was thought up by SETI pioneer Frank Drake. It is actually a fairly simple way of working out how many advanced civilizations might be around at any one time.

It is guesswork, of course, and the number changes according to the values you put in.

N *Number of civilizations*
R *Rate of stars formed per year in our galaxy*
Fp *Fraction of stars with planets*
Np *Suitable planets per planetary system*
Fl *Fraction of planets on which life starts*
Fi *Fraction of life that evolves to intelligence*
Fc *Intelligent species that develop communication*
L *Number of years of technology*

So far, SETI researchers have not had any solid results, but there have been some 'near misses.' In 1977, equipment at Ohio State University picked up a strange signal from the direction of the constellation Sagittarius. It lasted just 37 seconds, but was so unusual that it was named the 'Wow!' signal, after the note written at the side of the computer printout. It was never repeated, however, and remains a total mystery. Other odd signals have come from much closer to home. For example, two British SETI researchers received strange signals in 1996 that turned out to be from a super-secret military satellite circling overhead in Earth's orbit.

The 'Wow!' signal of 1977 still baffles SETI researchers

Radio telescopes usually hunt for signals on the 'hydrogen line,' radio frequency. SETI researchers think this frequency is the one that ET's might use.

Today, there are several search projects underway, including that of the SETI League, an international group dedicated to building a planet-wide network of linked receivers. The League plans to have 5000 amateur receivers listening to all parts of the sky. The plan is called Project Argus, after the 100-eyed giant of ancient Greek mythology. The plan may be possible because of the falling price of computer equipment. Computers that cost a fortune back in the 1960s can now be assembled for the price of a used car. Using leftover parts, it is possible to put together an efficient SETI receiver system for even less.

Project Ozma was named after the queen of the magical kingdom in Frank Baum's famous book, The Wizard of Oz.

Are SETI researchers wasting their time? This is a question that cannot be answered yet, but not everyone regards their efforts as a hopeless cause.

▲ SETI researchers with computer equipment used to listen for space messages. If a genuine message from space comes, the International Astronomical Union and the United Nations will be told, and details will be sent to other scientists. No reply will be made until worldwide discussions take place.

Sending messages

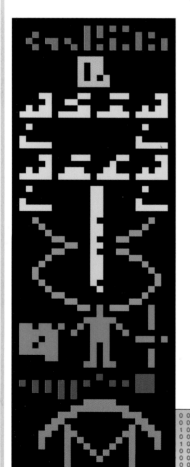

▲ *Star cluster M13, the target for greetings from Earth.*

SETI is not just about listening for signals. In 1974, a radio message from Earth was beamed out into deep space.

The message was sent by the 1000 ft (300 m) radio telescope at Arecibo, Puerto Rico. A team headed by two astronomers, Carl Sagan and Frank Drake, came up with a message constructed in binary code. It consisted of a string of 1679 characters, a stream of 'zeros' and 'ones' that, if decoded, come out as an unexpected pattern. It was a message designed to tell extraterrestrials something about us.

▶ *The Arecibo radio telescope lies in the mountains of the Caribbean island of Puerto Rico. Despite its large size, the aluminum panels of the bowl are very accurately assembled.*

◀ *The Arecibo message, shown here in color for clarity, includes:*
★ *Numbers 1-10 (red)*
★ *Chemicals (orange)*
★ *Human biology information (yellow, green)*
★ *Human being (light blue)*
★ *Solar System (blue)*
★ *Arecibo telescope (purple)*

Sagan and Drake thought that intelligent aliens could work out that 1679 comes from multiplying the numbers 23 and 73, and, by laying these out as a grid, the signal turns into a picture. Working out the meaning of the puzzle diagrams is not easy, however, and some volunteer testers never did manage it!

On November 16, 1974, the message was beamed toward the star cluster M13 in the constellation of Hercules. We cannot expect an answer soon. M13 is about 25,000 light-years away. A reply will not arrive until the year 52,000 at the earliest.

◀ *The numbers make no sense until you lay them out as a grid. Then you see the diagrams shown far left.*

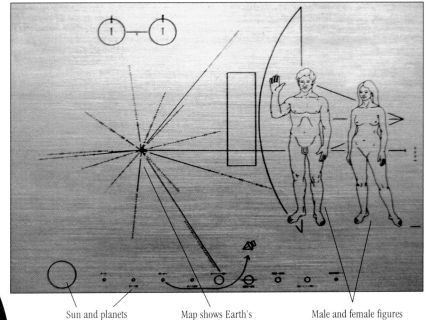

▶ Several space probes carry engraved plaques as a sort of 'message in a bottle' for intelligent ETs that may find them in the future. This one was placed aboard a Pioneer spacecraft. It includes diagrams of the Solar System, a man and woman in scale to the spacecraft, and a map showing Earth's position in space.

Sun and planets

Map shows Earth's position in space

Male and female figures

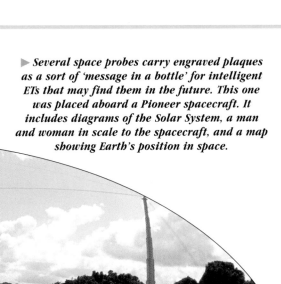

The message to M13 was the first powerful signal deliberately fired into space, but our planet has been broadcasting radio and television signals for years. Our radio 'noise,' from daily news to TV soap operas, is spreading out into the universe at the speed of light. ETs within 100 light-years of Earth could now be receiving the faint cracklings of early radio broadcasts.

The first TV programs are about 60 light-years out in space. ETs living on a planet near the star Alpha Centauri could be watching TV shows made on Earth just four years ago.

◀ Carl Sagan was one of the scientists behind the Arecibo signal.

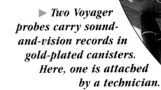

▶ Two Voyager probes carry sound-and-vision records in gold-plated canisters. Here, one is attached by a technician.

The UFO mystery

▲ *Kenneth Arnold's book describes his mid-air encounter.*

Some people think that we do not need to spend money on the SETI radio receiver program. They claim that alien spacecraft are already here.

The modern age of unidentified flying objects, better known as UFOs, began on June 24, 1947, when an American pilot, Kenneth Arnold, reported seeing shiny discs flying over the Cascade Mountains. He described them as moving at very high speed and skipping "like saucers across water." This was how the term 'flying saucer' was born, and it has been used many times over the years for almost any unknown flying object.

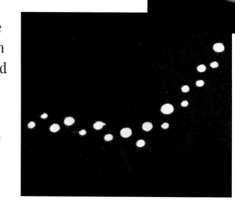

▲ *The brightly shining planet Venus (shown here in close-up view) is often mistaken for a UFO.*

▶ *This formation of night-flying geese showed up on radar as a 'UFO squadron.'*

▲ *The classic shape for a UFO is a domed saucer. Other shapes claimed by UFO-spotters include spheres, cigars, cylinders, and cones.*

Since Arnold's sighting, there have been many UFO reports made worldwide. Most can be explained as sightings of familiar things in the sky such as the planet Venus or a flight of geese.

Many sightings have been hoaxes, but a few, including Arnold's sighting, have no explanation. His saucers flew at over 1200 mph (1930 km/h), at a time when the world's fastest plane, the Bell X-1, could achieve only about half this speed.

The Bell X-1 was the world's fastest plane in 1947

▶ *Goblin-like 'Gray' aliens were said to be the crew of the Roswell UFO.*

▲ *The Roswell UFO incident was included in the storyline of the 1996 Hollywood movie 'Independence Day,' which showed ET invaders trying to take over the Earth. The movie's hero solved the riddle of how to fly a UFO in a few hours, defeating the enemy using his Apple computer. The 1997 movie 'Men in Black' was even less serious. Its heroes defended the Earth against the "scum of the universe," a delightful collection of weird and wonderful alien creatures!*

▶ *There have been thousands of UFO reports. In 1971, there was even a steam-iron shaped UFO spotted near Loch Ness, in Scotland! There are some similarities in all reports – UFOs move at high speed, starting and stopping so suddenly that a human astronaut would be squashed flat. They are also said to operate in a totally different way than any flying machine known on Earth.*

By the 1990s, TV shows and movies with 'alien' plot lines had become very popular. They reflected people's love of mysteries and the unknown. Despite many claims and stories there is no hard evidence that UFOs or alien astronauts exist or have ever visited Earth.

One story centers on a supposed UFO crash near Roswell, New Mexico, in 1947. A mystery spacecraft and crew were reported to have been found there by the U.S. military and whisked away to a secret 'Area 51' for experiments. The U.S. Pentagon published a four-year investigation, Roswell: Case Closed, which looked into every aspect of the case and dismissed the UFO as a deflated weather balloon. Despite this, believers still say that it is all a cover-up, and so the mystery remains.

What are close encounters?

Close encounters fall into several types, as first defined by UFO expert J. Allen Hynek. A close encounter of the first kind (CE1K) is when you see a UFO in the sky or on the ground. CE2K is when the UFO leaves evidence such as holes in the ground, or burn marks on buildings. The 1978 movie, 'Close Encounters of the Third Kind' (CE3K), featured contact with aliens. Most encounter evidence is limited to eye-witness accounts and blurred photos, with a lot of fakes. It is a fascinating subject, with people claiming thousands of sightings.

ETs vary in appearance. Most reports claim they have a humanoid shape, with head, two arms, and legs

Design an alien

Even if we find alien creatures, they may look weird to our eyes. Their appearance will have evolved through environmental factors on their home planet.

▲ *Inventing ETs is not new, as this cover from a magazine of the 1960s shows. The magazine featured a discussion on aliens by scientist Willy Ley.*

The basic materials that make up the living things on Earth, carbon, hydrogen, oxygen, and nitrogen, are scattered across the universe. Because of this, the possibilities for life in space are probably limitless.

▲ *Vicious creatures, as conceived for the 'Alien' movie series, lay eggs in hosts (like many insects do) and have acid blood.*

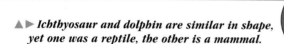

▲▶ *Ichthyosaur and dolphin are similar in shape, yet one was a reptile, the other is a mammal.*

There may be many planets with life, but an exact duplicate of Earth is unlikely to exist anywhere. Many things will be different on other planets, such as the length of a day and year, atmosphere, temperature, and climate. These factors could lead to dramatic changes in how life develops. On similar planets, familiar-looking creatures might exist. Here on Earth, present-day dolphins have a similar shape to prehistoric ichthyosaurs, which lived millions of years ago. Some living things on other planets may even have eyes, as do many animals on Earth, from the octopus to human beings.

▼ *Explorers from Earth touch down on a life-packed alien planet in this scene from a 1959 space adventure serial.*

Eye structures each span more than 3 ft (1 m)

Are giant insects likely?

Giant insect-type creatures are not impossible, but they are more likely to develop on a world with low gravity. Insects have a hard outer covering called an exoskeleton. Here on Earth, a 30 ft (10 m) ant would probably collapse under its own weight. On a world where weight is not such a problem, giant insects might exist.

Exoskeleton, made of a hard substance called chitin

Antenna

Huge ears catch faint sounds in thin atmosphere

Eyes and nose can fold away as protection against extreme cold at night

Huge, fur-covered lungs cope with low oxygen supply

S trange creatures might live on other planets. On a small planet with low gravity, for example, tree-type plants could soar to 650 ft (200 m) or more. A giraffe-like animal might have a neck twice as long as a giraffe on Earth. On a larger planet with a stronger gravity pull, the reverse might be the case, with short, squat plants and hefty animals with massive bones and large bodies.

It is unlikely that ETs that look like humans will exist, although some may have a 'humanoid' look. The upright, two-legged form, with eyes and ears on a swiveling head, plus a pair of upper limbs for handling things and using tools, is a good design for survival. It could develop in many environments.

▶ *An astronaut meets a Martian in this 1939 painting by Frank Paul. Martians like this almost certainly do not exist but the body design does reflect the planet's atmosphere.*

Suction-pad feet

Are we alone?

▲ *According to the 'protection' theory of extra-terrestrial life, aliens 'look after' humans.*

More than 30 years of searching has failed to find evidence of intelligent aliens, or other life forms in the universe.

Some experts think they know why SETI has failed to receive any messages. Frank Tipler, of Tulane University, New Orleans, thinks that there are no intelligent ETs to find, but he does believe primitive life may exist. According to Tipler, humans are probably the first intelligent beings in our galaxy. His theory is that there has been time for ETs to explore the galaxy, not just once but many times. Even slow space probes would take only about three million years to cross the Milky Way. Tipler's conclusion is that ETs have not arrived because they are not there in the first place.

▲ *Tipler has suggested that humanity really is alone, and therefore we should build life-sustaining environments on other planets. He believes Mars could be revived by adding oceans and atmosphere, using materials from some of the billions of water-ice comets drifting in space.*

There are some ET theories that are not based on any scientific evidence. One idea is the 'protection' theory. This science-fiction theory says humans are a simple form of life, and friendly ETs keep us isolated so that our development is not ruined by their super-civilization. The 'galactic zoo' science-fiction theory suggests humans are kept as pets, unaware of their keepers. Another theory suggests that aliens have not visited Earth because they have destroyed themselves in warfare.

◄ *An artist's creative illustration of an imaginary alien hunting for a meal.*

There is a possibility of finding simple life forms in the Solar System, with both Mars and Europa being likely sites. What about life elsewhere? Today, it is pure guesswork, but if Earth-like planets are found, the chances should improve.

So what about UFOs? Again, it is guesswork, but if they do exist, their secretive ways are in line with the 'zoo' or 'protection' theories. ETs may not even be friendly. In one old science-fiction story, aliens arrive with cures for human diseases and other problems. Soon, healthy people are invited to go on trips to distant planets. A dreadful secret is revealed when it turns out that the aliens' reading matter, To Serve Man, is really a cookbook!

▲ Discovery of life on other worlds could spark exploration fever. This future scene shows an imaginary Mars base, with a lifesearch team setting off in a sand cruiser.

► Some of the varied forms of life on a jungle world, designed by an artist in the early 1900s.

Time track

A look at some of the important dates and events in space exploration and the history of hunting for extraterrestrial life. Some science-fiction ideas about alien life are also listed.

▲ Humans find themselves prisoners of the Selenites, Moon dwellers in Jules Verne's 1901 book 'The First Men in the Moon.'

1516   Italian Lodovico Ariosto writes the epic poem Orlando Furioso, in which a journey to the Moon is made in a 'firie charret.' The Moon is found to be lifeless.

1543   Polish astronomer Nicolaus Copernicus publishes On the Revolutions of Heavenly Spheres, in which he suggests the Earth and planets go round the Sun.

1566   An artist's woodcut shows strange flying objects in the skies over the town of Basel, in Switzerland. It is thought to be an early UFO.

1600   Giordano Bruno is burned at the stake for suggesting that the universe might contain other inhabited worlds.

1608   Dutch optician Hans Lippershey constructs the first telescope.

1610   Italian astronomer Galileo Galilei sees four moons of Jupiter through his home-made telescope. His other discoveries include sunspots, rings of Saturn (though he cannot make out exactly what they are), and disc of Venus. Church authorities force him to deny the sightings are evidence of a Sun-centered planetary system. He is eventually placed under house arrest near Florence, where he continues his research until his death in 1642. Nearly 300 years later the Roman Catholic church accepts his discoveries.

1600s   More than 200 accounts of Moon voyages are published, mostly showing the moon inhabited by strange beings. One of the most famous books of the time is Somnium (Dream), a fantasy written by German astronomer Johannes Kepler.

1700s   Fiction goes hand-in-hand with scientific progress. Astronomy blossoms and English writer Jonathan Swift's Gulliver's Travels (1726) explores ideas about strange peoples and places.

1866   English writer H.G. Wells is born. His many stories include 'scientific romances,' such as The Time Machine (1895), War of the Worlds (1898) and The Shape of Things to Come (1933). With French writer Jules Verne, Wells is known as one of the 'fathers of science fiction.'

1876   U.S. writer Edgar Rice Burroughs is born. He becomes famous for his 'Tarzan' stories, but also writes science fiction, including tales set on 'Barsoom,' or Mars. For these stories, Burroughs invents warlike races, strange creatures, and beautiful princesses!

1877   Italian astronomer Giovanni Schiaparelli describes seeing canali, meaning furrows or channels, on the planet Mars. Although he never claims they are artificial, in English-speaking countries the word is taken to mean canals – and so the idea of a dying Martian civilization is born, with members of a doomed race digging vast canals to take water from the ice caps to desert areas. U.S. astronomer Percival Lowell takes up the idea and builds a laboratory at Flagstaff, Arizona, to study the skies. For over 20 years, he looks at Mars through the 24 inch (61 cm) telescope, writing that Mars has a "canal system embracing the whole planet."

1898   H.G. Wells writes The War of the Worlds, about a hostile race of Martians, keen to invade planet Earth.

1923   Edwin Hubble confirms that our Milky Way galaxy is just one of countless others, each a swirling island of stars in space. A typical galaxy, such as the Milky Way, contains about 100 billion stars.

1934   U.S. astronomer Carl Sagan is born. He helps create the SETI message sent by the Arecibo radio telescope in 1974. The Mars lander/rover of 1997 is named in his honor.

1947   Civilian U.S. pilot Kenneth Arnold claims to have seen nine wingless craft near Mt. Rainier in the Cascades. He describes them as "skipping like saucers would if you skipped them across water." The description is the origin of the popular term 'flying saucer.'

1959   SETI research is sparked off by an article in the science journal Nature by American scientists Giuseppe Cocconi and Philip Morrison. They point out that with radio equipment it should be possible to send and receive signals over long distances, even light-years. They also suggest a frequency to tune in to – it is the so-called 'hydrogen line,' the 8.3 in (21 cm) radiation emitted by hydrogen atoms, which are the most abundant in the universe.

1960   U.S. astronomer Frank Drake proposes the first large-scale SETI experiment. He equips an 85 ft (26 m) radio telescope at Green Bank, Virginia, with receiving gear that can detect signals from outer space. His plan, called Project Ozma, is approved. Drake targets the stars Epsilon Eridani and Tau Ceti. No signals are detected.

◄ Two fathers of science fiction, Jules Verne (left) and H.G. Wells.

1963   Dutch astronomer Peter van de Kamp is the first to claim evidence for a planet orbiting another star. His work is regarded by many astronomers as suspect, but spurs others to have a look. By 1976, van de Kamp has decided that Barnard's Star has two big planets.

1970   A Russian Venera probe lands on Venus, confirming that the planet's climate is far too hostile for life to survive.

1972   Space probes Pioneer 10 and 11 are launched into the Solar System on exploration missions. Each carries a gold-plated message plaque. Later, Voyager probes carry sounds and pictures on a disk. Dolphins and whales, Chuck Berry, Johann Sebastian Bach, and others are all sounds carried aboard. By the early 2000s, all these probes will be drifting far into interstellar space.

1974   A message is sent into space, aimed at the star cluster M13. The signal includes encoded pictures of humans and the Solar System. The message is sent on November 16 by the huge Arecibo radio telescope in Puerto Rico.

1976   Two Viking probes land on Mars, carrying lifesearch and other equipment. Some odd readings indicate possible life, but most scientists think they are caused by chemical reactions.

1977   Jerry Ehman, professor at Ohio State University's 'Big Ear' radio telescope, spots a 37-second long 'Wow' signal. Ehman says it was "the kind that an intelligent civilization might generate." No more signals are picked up, despite 100 more searches of that part of the sky.

1987   The IRAS space observatory takes a picture of the star Beta Pictoris, revealing a disk of gas and dust thought to be a planetary system that is forming.

1991   Alex Wolszczan tracks two objects circling a star in the constellation of Virgo. These are the first confirmed planets outside our Solar System. However, the star is a pulsar, which gives out much deadly radiation.

1993   A major SETI program, the HRMS, or High Resolution Microwave Survey, is stopped by U.S. senators. Frank Drake has to raise private money under the new SETI Institute to carry on the search. As 'Project Phoenix,' it plans to survey 1000 nearby Sun-like stars.

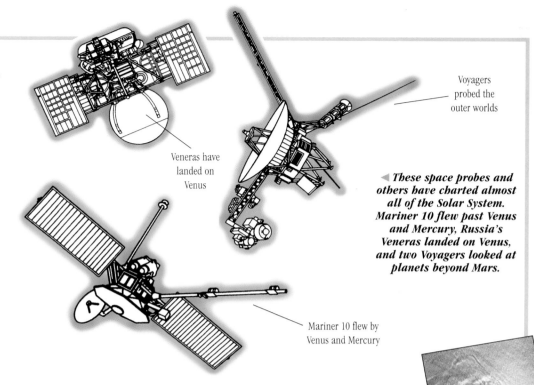

Veneras have landed on Venus

Voyagers probed the outer worlds

Mariner 10 flew by Venus and Mercury

◄ *These space probes and others have charted almost all of the Solar System. Mariner 10 flew past Venus and Mercury, Russia's Veneras landed on Venus, and two Voyagers looked at planets beyond Mars.*

1995   In France on October 6, Michel Mayor and Didier Queloz reveal details of a giant planet orbiting the star 51 Pegasi – the first such planet of a 'normal' star, similar to the Sun.

1996   In the U.S.A., Frank Tipler suggests that SETI is a waste of time since, if ETs exist, they would already be here.

1996   Claims are made that tiny structures in an Antarctic meteorite are fossils of dead Martian life. The claim is debated, and the matter remains open.

1997   The Hollywood movie Contact is released, based on a novel by award-winning physicist and astronomer Carl Sagan (1934-1996). The movie is welcomed by SETI researchers for bringing attention to their searches. Extra-terrestrials are not new to Hollywood. Earlier movies have included classics such as Close Encounters of the Third Kind and ET - The Extraterrestrial.

1997   Photographs of Jupiter's moon Europa by the Magellan space probe show that it may have oceans under ice.

1997   The Sojourner rover vehicle drives around on Mars. Its instruments confirm that the planet was probably much wetter in the distant past, so Mars may have had life at some point.

1998   The Hubble Space Telescope spots a possible giant planet orbiting the nearest star, Proxima Centauri.

1998   Mars Global Surveyor sends back pictures of the 'face' rock that show it is a natural formation and evidence for a dried-up ancient ocean in the north.

What is next ?

1999-2001 More probes land on Mars, checking for signs of simple organisms.

2004   The Huygens probe leaves the Cassini spacecraft and parachutes into Saturn's moon Titan's atmosphere. Its mission is to investigate chemicals thought to be like those on the early Earth.

2010   A robot probe is launched to investigate Jupiter's moon Europa for life signs. Drilling equipment and a mini-sub will explore under the icy surface.

2015   A high-power space telescope is placed in orbit beyond Jupiter to search for life.

▲ *The 'face' on Mars, as photographed in 1998 by Global Surveyor. From this angle, it appears to be a natural landscape feature.*

▼ *2001 Mars lander and rover vehicle.*

Glossary

An explanation of technical terms and concepts.

Amino acids
Units from which living organisms build up the proteins needed for tissues. In green plants, amino acids are made using carbon dioxide, water, and nitrogen, with energy supplied by sunlight. Animals need to eat nutrient-rich food. In 1957, it was discovered that amino acids could be formed by exposing a salt, ammonium acetate, to radiation. This discovery was a clue as to how life may have started.

Bell X-1
U.S. rocket plane, the first aircraft to fly at supersonic speed, in October 1947 by Charles Yeager. The speed of sound at high altitude is 660 mph (1,062 km/h). The X-1 was carried off the ground by a four-engine B-29 and dropped in mid-air, when the rocket motor could be fired.

Cepheid variable
A type of star that regularly brightens and fades slowly. The changing quality of its light allows astronomers to use such a star to check on distances in space.

Close encounter
A meeting with extraterrestrials; this comes in three stages, from seeing a UFO (Close Encounter of the First Kind, or CE1K); seeing one close up on the ground (CE2K); and actual contact with ETs (CE3K). The term was popularized by the Stephen Spielberg movie, Close Encounters of the Third Kind. Less well known is CE4K, closely associated with stories of abductions and experiments on humans by aliens for unknown purposes.

Comet
Comets are often described as 'dirty snowballs' in space. A comet is typically made of a frozen mixture of ice, dust and rock. Organic particles are part of the mixture, and one theory says comets colliding with the early Earth may have provided materials for life formation. Far away in space comets are dark and cold, but sometimes a comet passes near the Sun, and the heat starts to melt the icy nucleus. Soon the snowball is surrounded by a cloud of gas and dust, called the coma, which then stretches back away from the Sun to form gas and dust tails. Such a faintly-glowing tail is very thin indeed – it may be millions of miles long, yet you could pack all that material into a decent-size suitcase.

Constellation
One of 88 recognized 'star patterns' in the night skies, such as Taurus or Orion. They are not true groups of stars, but appear to be close together in our line of sight from Earth. They are a convenient way of dividing up the night sky.

Drake equation
A mathematical attempt by SETI pioneer Frank Drake to show how many other civilizations might be in our galaxy. According to Drake's sums, there may be thousands of ET civilizations out there.

Ecosphere
Zone around a star where water can exist on the surface of a planet as a liquid, making life as we know it possible. Today we think other places are possible, provided it is warm enough. Examples include the possible oceans beneath the icy surface of Saturn's moon Europa.

ET
Extraterrestrial (literally, 'away from the Earth'). Often used to describe an alien being.

Evolution
Theory that describes how today's complex living things developed from much simpler forms of life over millions of years.

Extinction
Complete disappearance of a species. May be because of natural causes, such as an Ice Age, or as a result of deliberate killing. The flightless dodo bird of Mauritius was hunted to extinction by sailors, for food. The last one was seen about 1680.

Extra-Solar
Beyond the Solar System.

Galaxy
Vast group of stars, turning slowly in space. They come in various shapes and sizes – spirals, barred, irregular and so on. A typical galaxy, such as our own Milky Way galaxy, may contain about 100 billion stars and is about 100,000 light-years across. There are thought to be 50 billion or more galaxies scattered through the universe.

Gray
Type of large-eyed extraterrestrial said to have been found at Roswell, New Mexico, in 1947.

Humanoid
Creature that is roughly human-shaped, having a single head, a body, two arms and two legs, all in about the right places.

Interstellar
Space between the stars. The universe is big. Whereas light from the Sun reaches Earth in just over eight minutes, light from the nearest other star (Proxima Centauri) takes more than four years to travel here.

Light-year
The distance travelled by light in one year at a speed of about 186,000 miles (300,000 km) per second .

M13
Globular star cluster, some 24,000 light-years from earth. The 'M' stands for Charles Messier (1730-1817) a French astronomer who listed 103 faint sky objects. Astronomers still name them using Messier's Catalogue numbers. Today, however, there are four items 'missing' from the list. They may have been comets that have since disappeared back into the outer Solar System.

Moon
Smaller companion to a planet. Earth's Moon is a cratered sphere 2,160 miles (3,476 km) across. Mars has two small lumpy moons, Phobos and Deimos, only a few miles across. The giant outer planets each have many more moons.

Nebula
Cloud-like region of gas and dust in the sky. Some are dark, others glow faintly. They are lit by young stars inside them.

Orbit
Curving path one space body takes around another. A spacecraft in low orbit circles the Earth about every 80 minutes. The Moon orbits the Earth once every 27.3 days. The Earth and the Moon together orbit the Sun once a year, or 365.3 days.

Protein
The main substance in a living cell, made up of amino acid units. There are thousands of types of proteins, depending on the different arrangements of the amino acid 'building blocks.'

▶ This type of radio telescope uses a big dish to concentrate faint signals into a receiving antenna. The dish is mounted on three arms at the top of the picture. The dish itself can be steered very precisely to track objects as they move in space.

Proxima Centauri
The nearest star to our Solar System, just over four light-years away. The Centauri star system has two other stars, Alpha and Beta Centauri, and at least one planet – a gas giant orbiting Proxima.

Radio telescope
Type of telescope that detects radio emissions from space, rather than light for photography. As light is only a tiny part of the electromagnetic spectrum, radio telescopes can actually 'see' far more than an optical telescope.

SETI
Search for ExtraTerrestrial Intelligence.

Single-cell organism
The cell is the basic living unit of all plants and animals, and a single-cell organism is the simplest form of life. Most organisms are made of millions of cells, arranged into tissues and organs.

Solar System
The Sun, together with the planets, moons, comets, rocks, dust and other debris that circle it. Other systems are known to exist, although a planet like Earth has yet to be discovered.

Surveyor probe
One of many U.S. space probes that mapped the Moon before the manned Apollo missions were sent to land there. Five Surveyors landed on the Moon.

UFO
Unidentified Flying Object. Term for any strange object seen in the sky, although it is used mostly when talking about possible alien spacecraft.

Volcanic vent
Crack or hole in the sea floor from which heat and gases escape from an underwater volcano. On Earth, many strange creatures have been found living around such vents, including worms seven feet (2 m) long. Basic foods for these lifeforms are bacteria, which in turn thrive on hydrogen sulphide in the gas bubbling from the vent.

▼ Disks in space – new planetary systems forming in the constellation of Orion. Sizes range from twice our own Solar System to a giant seventeen times as big.

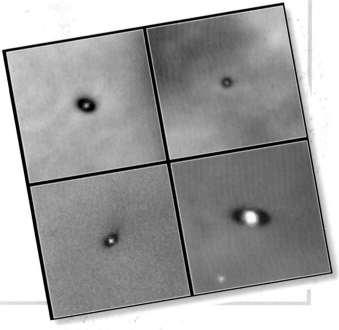

Index

Acknowledgements
We wish to thank all those individuals and
organizations that have helped create this
publication.

Photographs were supplied by:
Alan West
Alpha Archive
Ball Aerospace
Bruce Coleman Collection
Corbis
Hubble Space Telescope Images
Mat Irvine/Small Space Photos
JPL Jet Propulsion Laboratory
KPT Images
Natural History Museum
Science Photo Library
NASA Space Agency

Digital art created by:
David Hardy
Nick Witte-Vermeulen
Rory McLeish
David Jefferis
Tom Granberg 'Renderbrandt'